Prof. Dr. Gretchen James

BUSINESS GENIUS

Genius Persuasion

BY

Prof. Dr. Gretchen James

BUSINESS GENIUS

Copyright@2022Prof. Dr. Gretchen James

Al Rights Reserved

Prof. Dr. Gretchen James

TABLE OF CONTENT

INTRODUCTION 4
CHAPTER ONE 6
   MARKET RESEARCH AND COMPETITIVE ANALYSIS 6
- Questionnaires 9
  - Use competitive analysis to find a market advantage 9
  - Free small business data and trends 11

CHAPTER TWO 12
   FUND YOUR BUSINESS 12
      Get venture capital from investors 13
      How to get venture capital funding 14
      Find an investor 14
      1. Share your business plan 15
      2. Go through due diligence review 15
      3. Work out the terms 15
      Investment 16
      Get a small business loan 17
   Use Lender Match to find lenders who offer SBA-guaranteed loans 18
      Small Business Investment Company (SBIC) 19
      Small Business Innovation Research (SBIR) program 19
      Small Business Technology Transfer (STTR) program 20

CHAPTER THREE 22
   CHOOSE A BUSINESS STRUCTURE 22
      Review common business structures 23
         Sole proprietorship 23
         Partnership 24

Limited liability company (LLC)	26
Corporation	27
S corp	29
Close corporation	31
Nonprofit corporation	32
Cooperative	33
Combine different business structures	34
Compare business structures	34
CHAPTER FOUR	36
CHOOSE YOUR BUSINESS NAME	36
Trademark	37
Doing business as (DBA) name	38
CHAPTER FIVE	40
PICK YOUR BUSINESS LOCATION	40
Research the best place to locate your business	40
Local zoning ordinances	41
State and local government incentives	42
Federal Government Incentives	43
Doing business as (DBA) name	43
CHAPTER SIX	46
REGISTER YOUR BUSINESS	46
Register with state agencies	47
Get a registered agent	48
File for foreign qualification	49
File state documents and fees	51
Register with local agencies	51
Stay up to date with registration requirements	52

Prof. Dr. Gretchen James

CHAPTER SEVEN..54

    OPEN A BUSINESS BANK ACCOUNT 54

    Benefits of business bank accounts As soon as you start accepting or spending money as your business, you should open a business bank account. Common business accounts include a checking account, savings account, credit card account, and a merchant services account. Merchant services accounts allow you to accept credit and debit card transactions from your customers. 54

    Find an account with low fees and good benefits. Some business owners open a business account at the same bank they use for their personal accounts. Rates, fees, and options vary from bank to bank, so you should shop around to make sure you find the lowest fees and the best benefits. 56

    Get documents you need to open a business bank account........................58

    CONCLUSION 60

INTRODUCTION

Market research helps you find customers for your business. Competitive analysis helps you make your business unique. Combine them to find a competitive advantage for your small business. The business structure you choose influences everything from day-to-day operations, to taxes and how much of your personal assets are at risk. You should choose a business structure that gives you the right balance of legal protections and benefits.

Your business location determines the taxes, zoning laws, and regulations your business will be subject to. You'll need to make a strategic decision about which state, city, and neighborhood you choose to start your business in.

Prof. Dr. Gretchen James

You can find the right business name with creativity and market research. Once you've picked your name, you should protect it by registering it with the right agencies.

CHAPTER ONE

MARKET RESEARCH AND COMPETITIVE ANALYSIS

Market research blends consumer behavior and economic trends to confirm and improve your business idea.

It's crucial to understand your consumer base from the outset. Market research lets you reduce risks even while your business is still just a gleam in your eye.

Gather demographic information to better understand opportunities and limitations for gaining customers. This could include population data on age, wealth, family, interests, or anything else that's relevant for your business.

Then answer the following questions to get a good sense of your market:

Demand: Is there a desire for your product or service?

Market size: How many people would be interested in your offering?

Economic indicators: What is the income range and employment rate?

Location: Where do your customers live and where can your business reach?

Market saturation: How many similar options are already available to consumers?

Pricing: What do potential customers pay for these alternatives?

You'll also want to keep up with the latest small business trends. It's important to gain a sense of the specific market share that will impact your profits.

You can do market research using existing sources, or you can do the research yourself and go direct to consumers.

Existing sources can save you a lot of time and energy, but the information might not be as specific to your audience as you'd like. Use it to answer questions that are both general and quantifiable, like industry trends, demographics, and household incomes. Check online or start with our list of market research resources.

Asking consumers yourself can give you a nuanced understanding of your specific target audience. But, direct research can be time consuming and expensive. Use it to answer questions about your specific business or customers, like reactions to your logo, improvements you could make to buying experience, and where customers might go instead of your business.

Prof. Dr. Gretchen James

Here are a few methods you can use to do direct research:

- Surveys
- Questionnaires
- Focus groups
- In-depth interviews

For guidance on deciding which methods are worthwhile for your small business, the U.S. Small Business Administration (SBA) provides counseling services through our resource partner network.

Use competitive analysis to find a market advantage

Competitive analysis helps you learn from businesses competing for your potential customers. This is key to defining a competitive edge that creates sustainable revenue.

Your competitive analysis should identify your competition by product line or service and market segment. Assess the following characteristics of the competitive landscape:

- Market share
- Strengths and weaknesses
- Your window of opportunity to enter the market
- The importance of your target market to your competitors
- Any barriers that may hinder you as you enter the market
- Indirect or secondary competitors who may impact your success

Several industries might be competing to serve the same market you're targeting. The Department of Justice provides a diagram of Porter's Five Forces as one way you

Prof. Dr. Gretchen James

can differentiate your competitive analysis by industry. Important factors to consider include level of competition, threat of new competitors or services, and the effect of suppliers and customers on price.

Free small business data and trends

There are many reliable sources that provide customer and market information at no cost. Free statistics are readily available to help prospective small business owners.

CHAPTER TWO

FUND YOUR BUSINESS

Your personal financial situation and vision for your business will shape the financial future of your business. Once you know how much startup funding you'll need, it's time to figure out how you'll get it. Otherwise known as bootstrapping, self-funding lets you leverage your own financial resources to support your business. Self-funding can come in the form of turning to family and friends for capital, using your savings accounts, or even tapping into your 401(k). With self-funding, you retain complete control over the business, but you also take on all the risk yourself. Be careful not to spend more than you can afford, and be especially careful if you choose to tap into retirement accounts early. You might face expensive fees or penalties, or damage your ability to retire on time — so you should check with your plan's administrator and a personal financial advisor first.

Get venture capital from investors

Investors can give you funding to start your business in the form of venture capital investments. Venture capital is normally offered in exchange for an ownership share and active role in the company.

Venture capital differs from traditional financing in a number of important ways. Venture capital typically:

- Focuses high-growth companies
- Invests capital in return for equity, rather than debt (it's not a loan)

- Takes higher risks in exchange for potential higher returns
- Has a longer investment horizon than traditional financing

Almost all venture capitalists will, at a minimum, want a seat on the board of directors. So be prepared to give up some portion of both control and ownership of your company in exchange for funding.

How to get venture capital funding

There's no guaranteed way to get venture capital, but the process generally follows a standard order of basic steps.

Find an investor

Look for individual investors — sometimes called "angel investors" — or venture capital firms. Be sure to do enough background research to know if the investor is reputable and has experience working with startup companies.

1. **Share your business plan**

   The investor will review your business plan to make sure it meets their investing criteria. Most investment funds concentrate on an industry, geographic area, or stage of business development.

2. **Go through due diligence review**

   The investors will look at your company's management team, market, products and services, corporate governance documents, and financial statements.

3. **Work out the terms**

   If they want to invest, the next step is to agree on a term sheet that describes the terms and conditions for the fund to make an investment.

Investment

Once you agree on a term sheet, you can get the investment! Once a venture fund has invested, it becomes actively involved in the company. Venture funds normally come in "rounds." As the company meets milestones, further rounds of financing are made available, with adjustments in price as the company executes its plan.

Crowd funding raises funds for a business from a large number of people, called crowd funders. Crowd funders aren't technically investors, because they don't receive a share of ownership in the business and don't expect a financial return on their money.

Instead, crowd funders expect to get a "gift" from your company as thanks for their contribution. Often, that gift is the product you plan to sell or other special perks, like meeting the business owner or getting their name in the credits. This makes crowd funding a popular option for people who want to produce creative works (like a documentary), or a physical product (like a high-tech cooler).

Crowd funding is also popular because it's very low risk for business owners. Not only do you get to retain full control of your company, but if your plan fails, you're typically under no obligation to repay your crowd funders. Every crowd funding platform is different, so make sure to read the fine print and understand your full financial and legal obligations.

Get a small business loan

If you want to retain complete control of your business, but don't have enough funds to start, consider a small business loan.

To increase your chances of securing a loan, you should have a business plan, expense sheet, and financial projections for the next five years. These tools will give you an idea of how much you'll need to ask for, and will help the bank know they're making a smart choice by giving you a loan.

Once you have your materials ready, contact banks and credit unions to request a loan. You'll want to compare offers to get the best possible terms for your loan.

Use Lender Match to find lenders who offer SBA-guaranteed loans

Prof. Dr. Gretchen James

If you have trouble getting a traditional business loan, you should look into SBA-guaranteed loans. When a bank thinks your business is too risky to lend money to, the U.S. Small Business Administration (SBA) can agree to guarantee your loan. That way, the bank has less risk and is more willing to give your business a loan.

Small Business Investment Company (SBIC)

SBICs are privately owned and managed investment funds licensed and regulated by SBA. They use their own capital, plus funds borrowed with an SBA guarantee, to make equity and debt investments in qualifying small businesses. Learn more about SBICs to see if your business might qualify.

Small Business Innovation Research (SBIR) program

This program encourages small businesses to engage in federal research and development that has the potential for commercialization. Find out if the SBIR's competitive awards-based program makes sense for you.

Small Business Technology Transfer (STTR) program
This program offers funding opportunities in the federal innovation research and development arena. Small businesses who qualify for this program work with nonprofit research institutions in the early and intermediate stages of starting up. Find out if the STTR program makes sense for your business.

Prof. Dr. Gretchen James

CHAPTER THREE

CHOOSE A BUSINESS STRUCTURE

- Review common business structures
- Combine different business structures
- Compare business structures

Your business structure affects how much you pay in taxes, your ability to raise money, the paperwork you need to file, and your personal liability.

You'll need to choose a business structure before you register your business with the state. Most businesses will also need to get a tax ID number and file for the appropriate licenses and permits.

Choose carefully. While you may convert to a different business structure in the future, there may be restrictions based on your location. This could also result in tax consequences and unintended dissolution, among other complications.

Consulting with business counselors, attorneys, and accountants can prove helpful.

Review common business structures

Sole proprietorship

A sole proprietorship is easy to form and gives you complete control of your business. You're automatically considered to be a sole proprietorship if you do business activities but don't register as any other kind of business.

Sole proprietorships do not produce a separate business entity. This means your business assets and liabilities are not separate from your personal assets and liabilities. You can be held personally liable for the debts and obligations of the business. Sole proprietors are still able to get a trade name. It can also be hard to raise money because you can't sell stock, and banks are hesitant to lend to sole proprietorships.

Sole proprietorships can be a good choice for low-risk businesses and owners who want to test their business idea before forming a more formal business.

Partnership

Partnerships are the simplest structure for two or more people to own a business together. There are two common kinds of partnerships: limited partnerships (LP) and limited liability partnerships (LLP).

Limited partnerships have only one general partner with unlimited liability, and all other partners have limited

Prof. Dr. Gretchen James

liability. The partners with limited liability also tend to have limited control over the company, which is documented in a partnership agreement. Profits are passed through to personal tax returns, and the general partner — the partner without limited liability — must also pay self-employment taxes.

Limited liability partnerships are similar to limited partnerships, but give limited liability to every owner. An LLP protects each partner from debts against the partnership, they won't be responsible for the actions of other partners.

Partnerships can be a good choice for businesses with multiple owners, professional groups (like attorneys), and groups who want to test their business idea before forming a more formal business.

Limited liability company (LLC)

An LLC lets you take advantage of the benefits of both the corporation and partnership business structures.

LLCs protect you from personal liability in most instances, your personal assets — like your vehicle, house, and savings accounts — won't be at risk in case your LLC faces bankruptcy or lawsuits.

Profits and losses can get passed through to your personal income without facing corporate taxes. However, members of an LLC are considered self-employed and must pay self-employment tax contributions towards Medicare and Social Security.

LLCs can have a limited life in many states. When a member joins or leaves an LLC, some states may require the LLC to be dissolved and re-formed with new membership —unless there's already an agreement in place within the LLC for buying, selling, and transferring ownership.

LLCs can be a good choice for medium- or higher-risk businesses, owners with significant personal assets they want protected, and owners who want to pay a lower tax rate than they would with a corporation.

Corporation

C corp

A corporation, sometimes called a C corp, is a legal entity that's separate from its owners. Corporations can make a profit, be taxed, and can be held legally liable.

Corporations offer the strongest protection to its owners from personal liability, but the cost to form a corporation is higher than other structures. Corporations also require more extensive record-keeping, operational processes, and reporting.

Unlike sole proprietors, partnerships, and LLCs, corporations pay income tax on their profits. In some cases, corporate profits are taxed twice — first, when the company makes a profit, and again when dividends are paid to shareholders on their personal tax returns.

Corporations have a completely independent life separate from its shareholders. If a shareholder leaves the company or sells his or her shares, the C corp can continue doing business relatively undisturbed.

Prof. Dr. Gretchen James

Corporations have an advantage when it comes to raising capital because they can raise funds through the sale of stock, which can also be a benefit in attracting employees.

Corporations can be a good choice for medium- or higher-risk businesses, those that need to raise money, and businesses that plan to "go public" or eventually be sold.

S corp

An S corporation, sometimes called an S corp, is a special type of corporation that's designed to avoid the double taxation drawback of regular C corps. S corps allow profits, and some losses, to be passed through directly to owners' personal income without ever being subject to corporate tax rates. Not all states tax S corps equally, but most recognize them the same way the federal government does and tax the shareholders accordingly. Some states tax S corps on profits above a specified limit and other states don't recognize the S corp election at all, simply treating the business as a C corp. S corps must file with the IRS to get S corp status, a different process from registering with their state. There are special limits on S corps. Check the IRS website for eligibility requirements. You'll still have to follow the strict filing and operational processes of a C corp. S corps also have an independent life, just like C corps. If a shareholder leaves the company or sells his or her shares, the S corp can continue doing business relatively undisturbed. S corps can be a good choice for a businesses that would otherwise be a C corp, but meet the criteria to file as an S corp.

Prof. Dr. Gretchen James

B corp

A benefit corporation, sometimes called a B corp, is a for-profit corporation recognized by a majority of U.S. states. B corps are different from C corps in purpose, accountability, and transparency, but aren't different in how they're taxed. B corps are driven by both mission and profit. Shareholders hold the company accountable to produce some sort of public benefit in addition to a financial profit. Some states require B corps to submit annual benefit reports that demonstrate their contribution to the public good. There are several third-party B corp certification services, but none are required for a company to be legally considered a B corp in a state where the legal status is available.

Close corporation

Close corporations resemble B corps but have a less traditional corporate structure. These shed many formalities that typically govern corporations and apply to smaller companies. State rules vary, but shares are usually barred from public trading. Close corporations can be run by a small group of shareholders without a board of directors.

Nonprofit corporation

Nonprofit corporations are organized to do charity, education, religious, literary, or scientific work. Because their work benefits the public, nonprofits can receive tax-exempt status, meaning they don't pay state or federal income taxes on any profits it makes. Nonprofits must file with the IRS to get tax exemption, a different process from registering with their state. Nonprofit corporations need to follow organizational rules very similar to a regular

C corp. They also need to follow special rules about what they do with any profits they earn. For example, they can't distribute profits to members or political campaigns. Nonprofits are often called 501(c)(3) corporations — a reference to the section of the Internal Revenue Code that is most commonly used to grant tax-exempt status.

Cooperative

A cooperative is a business or organization owned by and operated for the benefit of those using its services. Profits and earnings generated by the cooperative are distributed among the members, also known as user-owners. Typically, an elected board of directors and officers run the cooperative while regular members have voting power to control the direction of the cooperative. Members can become part of the cooperative by purchasing shares, though the amount of shares they hold does not affect the weight of their vote.

Combine different business structures

Designations like S corp and nonprofit aren't strictly business structures — they can also be understood as a tax status. It's possible for an LLC to be taxed as a C corp, S corp, or a nonprofit. These arrangements are far less common and can be more difficult to set up. If you're considering one of these non-standard structures, you should speak with a business counselor or an attorney to help you decide.

Compare business structures

Compare the general traits of these business structures, but remember that ownership rules, liability, taxes, and filing

Prof. Dr. Gretchen James

requirements for each business structure can vary by state. The following table is intended only as a guideline. Please confer with a business tax specialist to confirm your specific business needs.

CHAPTER FOUR

CHOOSE YOUR BUSINESS NAME

You'll want to choose a business name that reflects your brand identity and doesn't clash with the types of goods and services you offer.

Once you settle on a name you like, you need to protect it. There are four different ways to register your business name. Each way of registering your name serves a different purpose, and some may be legally required depending on your business structure and location.

- Entity name protects you at a state level
- Trademark protects you at a federal level
- Doing business as (DBA) doesn't give legal protection, but it might be legally required

- Domain name protects your business website address

Each of these name registrations are legally independent. Most small businesses try to use the same name for each kind of registration, but you're not normally required to.

Trademark

A trademark can protect the name of your business, goods, and services at a national level. Trademarks prevent others in the same (or similar) industry in the United States from using your trademarked names.

For example, if you were an electronics company and wanted to call your business Springfield Electronic Accessories and one of your products Screen Cover 5000, trademarking those names would prevent other electronics businesses or similar products from using those same names.

Businesses in every state are subject to trademark infringement lawsuits, which can prove costly. That's why you should check your prospective business, product, and service names against the official trademark database, maintained by the United States Patent and Trademark Office.

Doing business as (DBA) name

You might need to register your DBA — also known as a trade name, fictitious name, or assumed name — with the state, county, or city your business is located in. Registering your DBA name doesn't provide legal protection by itself, but most states require you to register your DBA if you use one. Some business structures require you to use a DBA.

Even if you're not required to register a DBA, you might want to anyway. A DBA lets you conduct business under a

Prof. Dr. Gretchen James

different identity from your own personal name or your formal business entity name. As an added bonus, getting a DBA and federal tax ID number (EIN) allows you to open a business bank account.

Multiple businesses can go by the same DBA in one state, so you're less restricted in what you can choose. There's also more leeway in the clarity of business function. For example, a small business owner could use Springfield Electronic Accessories for their entity name but use TechBuddy for their DBA. Just remember that trademark infringement laws will still apply.

Determine your DBA requirements based on your specific location. Requirements vary by business structure as well as by state, county, and municipality, so check with local government offices and websites.

CHAPTER FIVE

PICK YOUR BUSINESS LOCATION

You'll need to register your business, pay taxes, and get licenses and permits in the place you choose to locate your business. Where you locate your business depends in part on the location of your target market, business partners, and your personal preferences. In addition, you should consider the costs, benefits, and restrictions of different government agencies.

Research the best place to locate your business

When you calculate your startup costs, take into account the way different expenses might cost more or less depending on your location. Costs that can vary significantly by location include standard salaries, minimum wage laws, property values, rental rates, business insurance rates, utilities, and government licenses and fees.

Local zoning ordinances

If you buy, rent, build, or plan to work out of a physical property for your business, make sure it conforms to local zoning requirements.

Neighborhoods are generally zoned for either commercial or residential use. Zoning ordinances can restrict or entirely ban specific kinds of businesses from operating in an area.

You might have fewer zoning restrictions if you base your business out of your home, but zoning ordinances can still apply even to home-based businesses.

Zoning laws are typically controlled at the local level, so check with your department of city planning, or similar office, to find out about the zoning laws in your area. Consider the tax landscape for the state, county, and city. Income tax, sales tax, property tax, and corporate taxes can vary significantly from place to place. In fact, some states are well-known for creating tax environments that are very friendly to certain kinds of companies. That's part of the reason why tech startups, financial institutions, and manufacturing tend to concentrate in certain areas of the country. Visit state and local government websites to find out what the tax landscape for your area looks like.

State and local government incentives

Some state and local governments offer special tax credits for small businesses. You might also find state-specific small business loans or other financial incentives.

Incentive programs and benefits are often related to job creation, energy efficiency, urban redevelopment, and technology.

Visit local SBA Offices, Small Business Development Centers, Women's Business Centers state and local government websites to find more information.

Federal Government Incentives

The federal government offers benefits to small businesses that contract with the government and are based in underutilized areas. Check into the Historically Underutilized Business Zones (HUBZone) program to see if you qualify for preferential access to federal procurement opportunities.

Doing business as (DBA) name

You might need to register your DBA — also known as a trade name, fictitious name, or assumed name — with the state, county, or city your business is located in. Registering your DBA name doesn't provide legal protection by itself, but most states require you to register your DBA if you use one. Some business structures require you to use a DBA.

Even if you're not required to register a DBA, you might want to anyway. A DBA lets you conduct business under a different identity from your own personal name or your formal business entity name. As an added bonus, getting a DBA and federal tax ID number (EIN) allows you to open a business bank account. Multiple businesses can go by the same DBA in one state, so you're less restricted in what you can choose. There's also more leeway in the clarity of business function. For example, a small business owner

Prof. Dr. Gretchen James

could use Springfield Electronic Accessories for their entity name but use TechBuddy for their DBA. Just remember that trademark infringement laws will still apply. Determine your DBA requirements based on your specific location. Requirements vary by business structure as well as by state, county, and municipality, so check with local government offices and websites.

CHAPTER SIX

REGISTER YOUR BUSINESS

Register your business to make it a distinct legal entity. How and where you need to register depends on your business structure and business location. Your location and business structure determine how you'll need to register your business. Determine those factors first, and registration becomes very straightforward. For most small businesses, registering your business is as simple as registering your business name with state and local governments. In some cases, you don't need to register at all. If you conduct business as yourself using your legal name, you won't need to register anywhere. But remember, if you don't register your business, you could miss out on personal liability protection, legal benefits, and tax benefits. Most businesses don't need to register with the federal government to become a legal entity, other than simply filing to get a federal tax ID. Small businesses sometimes register with the federal government for trademark protection or tax exempt status. If you want to trademark your business, brand or product name, file with the United States Patent and Trademark office once you've formed your business. If you want tax-exempt status for a nonprofit corporation, register your business as a tax-exempt entity with the IRS. To create an S corp, you'll need to file form 2553 with the IRS.

Register with state agencies

If your business is a limited liability company (LLC), corporation, partnership, or nonprofit corporation, you'll probably need to register with any state where you conduct business activities.

Typically, you're considered to be conducting business activities in a state when:

- Your business has a physical presence in the state
- You often have in-person meetings with clients in the state
- A significant portion of your company's revenue comes from the state
- Any of your employees work in the state

Some states allow you to register online, and some states make you file paper documents in person or through the mail.

Most states require you to register with the Secretary of State's office, a Business Bureau, or a Business Agency.

Get a registered agent

If your business is an LLC, corporation, partnership, or nonprofit corporation, you'll need a registered agent in your state before you file.

A registered agent receives official papers and legal documents on behalf of your company. The registered agent must be located in the state where you register.

Many business owners prefer to use a registered agent service rather than take on this role themselves.

File for foreign qualification

If your LLC, corporation, partnership, or nonprofit corporation conducts business activities in more than one state, you might need to form your business in one state and then file for foreign qualification in other states where your business is active.

The state where you form your business will consider your business to be domestic, while every other state will view your business as foreign. Foreign qualification notifies the state that a foreign business is active there.

Foreign qualified businesses typically need to pay taxes and annual report fees in both their state of formation and states where they're foreign qualified.

To foreign qualify, file a Certificate of Authority with the state. Many states also require a Certificate of Good Standing from your state of formation. Each state charges a filing fee, but the amount varies by state and business structure.

Check with state offices to find out foreign qualification requirements and fees.

Prof. Dr. Gretchen James

File state documents and fees

In most cases, the total cost to register your business will be less than $300, but fees vary depending on your state and business structure.

The information you'll need typically includes:

- Business name
- Business location
- Ownership, management structure, or directors
- Registered agent information
- Number and value of shares (if you're a corporation)

The documents you need — and what goes in them — will vary based on your state and business structure.

Register with local agencies

Typically, you don't need to register with county or city governments to actually form your business. If your business is an LLC, corporation, partnership, or nonprofit corporation, you might need to file for licenses and permits from the county or city. Some counties and cities also require you to register your DBA — a trade name or a fictitious name — if you use one. Local governments determine registration, licensing, and permitting requirements, so visit local government websites to find out what you need to do.

Stay up to date with registration requirements

Some states require you to provide reports soon after registering depending on your business structure. You may need to file additional documentation with your state tax board or franchise tax board. These filings are typically

Prof. Dr. Gretchen James

referred to as Initial Reports or Tax Board registration, and most often need to be filed within 30-90 days after you register with the state. Check with your local tax office or franchise tax board, if it applies to you.

CHAPTER SEVEN

OPEN A BUSINESS BANK ACCOUNT

Open a business account when you're ready to start accepting or spending money as your business. A business bank account helps you stay legally compliant and protected. It also provides benefits to your customers and employees

Benefits of business bank accounts As soon as you start accepting or spending money as your business, you should open a business bank account. Common business accounts include a checking account, savings account, credit card account, and a merchant services account. Merchant services accounts allow you to accept credit and debit card transactions from your customers.

You can open a business bank account once you've gotten your federal EIN.

Most business bank accounts offer perks that don't come with a standard personal bank account.

- **Protection.** Business banking offers limited personal liability protection by keeping your business funds separate from your personal funds. Merchant services also offer purchase protection for your customers and ensures that their personal information is secure.
- **Professionalism.** Customers will be able to pay you with credit cards and make checks out to your business instead of directly to you. Plus, you'll be able to authorize employees to handle day-to-day banking tasks on behalf of the business.

- **Preparedness.** Business banking usually comes with the option for a line of credit for the company. This can be used in the event of an emergency, or if your business needs new equipment.
- **Purchasing power.** Credit card accounts can help your business make large startup purchases and help establish a credit history for your business.

Find an account with low fees and good benefits. Some business owners open a business account at the same bank they use for their personal accounts. Rates, fees, and options vary from bank to bank, so you should shop around to make sure you find the lowest fees and the best benefits.

Here are things to consider when you're opening a business checking or savings account:

- Introductory offers
- Interest rates for savings and checking
- Interest rates for lines of credit
- Transaction fees
- Early termination fees
- Minimum account balance fees

Here are things to consider when you're opening a merchant services account:

- **Discount rate**: The percentage charged for every transaction processed
- **Transaction fees**: The amount charged for every credit card transaction
- **Address Verification Service (AVS) fees**
- **ACH daily batch fees**: Fees charged when you settle credit card transactions for that day

- **Monthly minimum fees**: Fees charged if your business doesn't meet the minimum required transactions

Payment processing companies are an increasingly popular alternative to traditional merchant services accounts. Payment processing companies sometimes provide extra functionality, like accessories that let you use your phone to accept credit card payments. The fee categories that you need to consider will be similar to merchant services account fees. If you find a payment processor that you like, remember that you'll still need to connect it to a business checking account to receive payments.

Get documents you need to open a business bank account

Opening a business bank account is easy once you've picked your bank. Simply go online or to a local branch to begin the

Prof. Dr. Gretchen James

process. Here are some of the most common documents banks ask for when you open a business bank account. Some banks may ask for more.

- Employer Identification Number (EIN) (or a Social Security number, if you're a sole proprietorship)
- Your business's formation documents
- Ownership agreements
- Business license

CONCLUSION

Buying an existing business is exactly what it sounds like. The buyer typically takes over full ownership of the business. The largest advantage is having an existing blueprint that can include important factors like an established customer base, defined operating expenses, and fully trained employees. Regardless of business type, almost any kind of business could be bought or sold.

When you buy an existing business, you typically get complete control over its direction. However, with no set vision, infrastructure, or external guidance, your business could struggle as you figure out the best way to run things.

Starting a business from scratch can be challenging. Franchising or buying an existing business can simplify the initial planning process.

Prof. Dr. Gretchen James

www.ingramcontent.com/pod-product-compliance
Lightning Source LLC
Chambersburg PA
CBHW070318220526
45465CB00004B/1892